I1052534

COLONIAL LIFE IN AMERICA

Troll Associates

COLONIAL LIFE IN AMERICA

by Louis Sabin

Illustrated by Hal Frenck

Troll Associates

Library of Congress Cataloging in Publication Data

Sabin, Louis.
    Colonial life in America.

    Summary: A brief look at colonial life in Jamestown
and in the New England settlements in the early seven-
teenth century.
    1. United States—Social life and customs—Colonial
period, ca. 1600-1775—Juvenile literature. [1. United
States—Social life and customs—Colonial period, ca.
1600-1775] I. Frenck, Hal, ill. II. Title.
E162.S2   1984   973.2   84-2669
ISBN 0-8167-0138-5 (lib. bdg.)
ISBN 0-8167-0139-3 (pbk.)

In the spring of 1607, three ships arrived in Virginia, and the first permanent English settlement was established in the New World. The colony, named Jamestown in honor of King James, was made up of about one hundred men. Their goals were to find a northwest passage to the Far East and to discover gold for shipment back to England.

Most of the Jamestown settlers were gentlemen who wore fine clothes and expected to be served by others. Others were craftsmen who were equally unprepared for the demands of the New World. There were only a few farmers, masons, and carpenters in the group, even though these were the kind of skilled workers a colony needed most.

During Jamestown's first two years, it became clear that the settlers had to adapt to the demands of the wilderness—or die. There was no gold and no northwest passage from Virginia. But there *was* land for farming. There were forests filled with trees for lumber. And there was plenty of game for food.

Those settlers who understood the situation followed the direction of their leader, Captain John Smith, and worked. But many did not, and times were hard.

Still more settlers came, until there were over five hundred colonists in Jamestown. Then, in the winter of 1609, a period the colonists called the "starving time," disease and starvation reduced their population to just fifty people.

An important lesson had been learned. Survival in the New World required hard work and a willingness to learn new ways. The colonists had to try to get along with their Indian neighbors and learn from them. Most of all, they had to learn to use the land and its resources.

The Jamestown settlers made peace with Chief Powhatan's tribe. They learned to raise corn as the Indians did. And John Rolfe, who married the chief's daughter, Pocahontas, introduced a kind of tobacco that would sell well in England. It came from the West Indies and grew as well in the rich Virginia soil as the tobacco that the Indians had always grown.

Finally, with the arrival of women and children from England, the settlement became a solid community. Jamestown's success firmly established the Virginia colony.

In each of the New England settlements that followed Jamestown, the same lessons had to be learned. Those settlers who adapted to the conditions of their new environment prospered. Those who tried to recreate England in America had great problems.

For example, the first settlers built houses like the ones they knew in England. They were made with clay, mud, brick, and stones and had thatched roofs. A thatched roof was good in the damp, cool climate of the British Isles. But it couldn't support the heavy snows of New England. And the thatches burned too easily after drying out in the New World climate.

It didn't take long for the sensible settlers to make changes. In the North that meant building wooden houses with sharply slanted, wood-shingle roofs that the snow would fall off. In the warm, sunny South that meant building homes with high-ceilinged rooms and large windows. This let in the cooling breezes and provided a place for the heat to rise.

The fireplace chimney, with its large cooking hearth, was set outside the framework of southern houses. This was done to keep the house cooler. Sometimes the cooking area was in a separate, small house next to the main house, to keep the heat completely away from the living quarters. In the North, however, the chimney was inside the framework of the house and was used for warmth as well as cooking.

In all phases of life, the key to success was adaptation. This was true for colonists of every class. In England, class structure was very rigid. People who were gentry—the highest level of society below royalty—were educated and unaccustomed to working with their hands.

In the middle class there were merchants, tradespeople, and farmers who owned land.

The class below them was made up of laborers, who worked on farms or in shops, and who owned no property. In England, these people seldom could rise above the class into which they were born. In the New World, they could and often did.

People from all three classes migrated to the colonies. Those who could pay for their passage did so. Those who could not pay came as indentured servants.

The indenture was a contract that said the master would pay for the passage. In return, the person had to work a few years on a farm, in a shop, in a house, in a mill, or however else the master chose.

After the indenture ended, the former servant was given farm land, tools to follow the craft that had been learned, or a job that paid wages. From then on, that person could rise as high in society as his or her skills and intelligence allowed.

Only slaves, brought from Africa, could not rise in colonial society. Even the slave who had been freed was not allowed the rights given to the rest of the colonists.

Except for the treatment of slaves, society in the New World was far more democratic than in England. Nearly all men who owned land or merchandise or farm animals could vote and could serve in the colonial legislatures.

Intelligence and the ability to speak persuasively were more important in these law-making bodies than wealth or family background. And many colonists without money or holdings became well-respected people because of their contributions to society.

It was easier to move up in society in the North than in the South. That is because most of the southern colonists were gentry with money, large plantations, and slaves. There were no jobs for poor settlers, because slaves provided free labor.

In the North, however, there was plenty of opportunity for the settlers to work. And a large number of colonists arrived in the New World determined to better their lives.

The Puritan religion in the North had a strong effect, too. Every member was expected to be active in the community. And everybody—rich and poor—was equal in the eyes of the church.

Furthermore, because the Bible was the heart of Puritanism, every Puritan had to be able to read it. So each New England community created a system of public education. Schooling wasn't free, but it cost very little, and the fee for poor children was often paid by the church.

For most colonial children, education ended at the age of twelve or thirteen. Only children of the very wealthy went on to college. After finishing grammar school, a boy usually became an apprentice, or assistant, to a local craftsman or merchant.

Apprenticeship generally lasted seven years. During that time the boy received food, clothing, a place to sleep, and training in his master's work. When he completed his apprenticeship, the young man became a journeyman. Now he was free to take a job for wages.

Many girls were apprenticed as needle-workers or house servants. Or a girl might stay at home and help in the house, in the store, or on the family farm until she married and set up her own house.

It took a lot of work to keep a colonial home going. Water had to be brought in from a well, and almost everything a family needed had to be made by members of the family.

The colonists, except those who were very rich, wore clothing they made themselves. People grew flax for linen and raised sheep for wool. The women then spun the yarn and wove it into cloth, which they cut and sewed into clothing. The colonists often made their own boots or shoes from tanned deer- and cowhides.

The colonists, including those who lived in the cities, raised much of their own food. They kept a vegetable garden, several chickens, pigs, and a dairy cow. Farm families, of course, raised far more food than they needed. They sold or traded the bulk of their crops to get the things they needed.

Cooking for a colonial family was a full-time job. There were always loaves of corn-

bread baking and pots of stew simmering in the big fireplace.

Most colonists ate all their meals at home. A breakfast of cornbread or porridge, and cold meat left over from the day before, started the day.

Dinner, the main meal, was served early in the afternoon. It consisted of hot bread or hasty pudding, which was boiled cornmeal. With that came a large stew of vegetables and meat, or a roast of meat or fowl made on a spit in the fireplace.

Other favorite dinner dishes were a pumpkin cooked whole, vegetables stewed in milk, applesauce and apple butter, fruit tarts, baked beans, cheeses, and eggs.

Supper in the evening was, like breakfast, usually a meal made up of leftovers and some hot corn pudding. Corn was the staple of the colonial diet.

Except for cooking pots and other metal tools, most colonial utensils were wooden and homemade. The same was true of furniture. The average colonial house had a large table for preparing and eating food, and a few rough chairs, stools, and benches. There was usually just one proper bed, which was for the parents. The children slept on sacks stuffed with straw, wool, or feathers in a loft above the main room.

In later colonial times, fine furniture was made by talented craftsmen. These pieces went into the large, elegant homes built for rich merchants and planters.

As the colonists adapted to the New World, the colonies grew very prosperous. The South exported cotton, rice, tobacco, and other money crops to England. The North exported fish, lumber, grain, and other farm goods.

The colonies imported manufactured goods from England, even though they could have made these things for themselves. But the English insisted on these rules of trade. This, and the high taxes imposed by the English, angered the colonists. More than one hundred years of colonial experience had convinced them that they could be self-sufficient.

The colonial experience did something else. The first settlers tried to create a world like the one they had left behind.

But that was impossible. So they changed their ways. Those who came after them, and the colonists' children, learned the new ways. These were strictly American.

The result was that, by the time the Revolutionary War began, the colonists were a separate people. Once they recognized this, the War of Independence was unavoidable. And when it came, it brought the colonial period to a close.